A Taste of
Chicken Soup for the Soul

Stories
of Faith

Inspirational Stories of Hope, Devotion,
Faith and Miracles

Jack Canfield
Mark Victor Hansen
Amy Newmark

CSS

Chicken Soup for the Soul Publishing, LLC
Cos Cob, CT

A Taste of Chicken Soup for the Soul Stories of Faith
Inspirational Stories of Hope, Devotion, Faith, and Miracles
by Jack Canfield, Mark Victor Hansen & Amy Newmark

Published by Chicken Soup for the Soul Publishing, LLC
www.chickensoup.com

Cover photos courtesy of © Radius Images/Alamy,
iStockphotos.com/sunnyfrog

Library of Congress Control Number: 2013940468

A Taste of ISBN: 978-1-61159-860-5
Full Book ISBN: 978-1-935096-14-6

Contents

How to be New and Different,

Bringing It to Pass, Football and All

There is no telling how many miles you will
have to run while chasing a dream.
~Author Unknown

It was a crisp fall day in Madison, Wisconsin, when our University of Wisconsin football team defeated the University of Illinois in the final Big Ten Conference home game of the season. Now Wisconsin was headed to the Hall of Fame Bowl in Tampa, Florida, over the Christmas holidays. My twenty-two-year-old son, Michael, a senior at University of Wisconsin at Madison, was a four-year member of their marching band, famous for their wildly entertaining high-stepping antics that dazzled crowds.

I'd desperately wanted to go to the Rose Bowl game the year before to watch him perform, but the trip was too expensive. I didn't know anyone in Pasadena to stay with, and airfare was out of the question. On New Year's Day 1994, my house was full of relatives as we all watched Michael on TV. He played his drums with such precision during the Rose Bowl parade and game that my heart nearly burst with excitement and pride.

When the Wisconsin Badgers won the right to play in the Hall of Fame Bowl the very next season, I realized that that game would be Michael's last time ever to march with the band before he graduated. I had to be there. Right!—a single parent with a small income and bigger-than-life dreams; that's me.

In late November, I mentioned my dream to my airline pilot friends who use the extra bedrooms in our home as their Milwaukee-area home away from home. One said he had a couple of low-cost "friend" passes that my fifteen-year-old son Andrew and I could use to get to Tampa and back.

"The passes are only about ninety dollars each, round-trip," he said. "But you'll have to fly standby."

I jumped at the chance as he set things in motion. Next, I had to find housing. I looked on the map and saw that our retired friends, Wally and Shirley, lived just forty-five minutes from Tampa. I was sure they'd put us up for the week in their Florida condo.

Everything seemed to be working smoothly until I called my dad in Illinois to tell him the good news. Dad planted my feet back on the ground when he said, "You're going to Florida between Christmas and New Year's? That's the busiest tourist week of the year down there! And you're flying standby? What do you think your chances are of getting on a plane that week?"

My bubble of optimism burst again when I

heard on the radio that nearly thirty thousand Wisconsinites had already bought tickets to the Hall of Fame Bowl. Our chances of getting down there flying standby certainly didn't look good. In fact, they looked impossible.

Besides, there was another glitch in the plans. The airline we'd be flying on had only one flight a day to Tampa. How could I even think there'd be empty seats on that plane during the week between Christmas and New Year's?

I told myself disgustedly, "How could you be so stupid? This will never work!"

In addition to decorating for Christmas, buying gifts, cleaning house and planning meals for the holidays, I now had an additional stressor in my life.

I commiserated with my friend Heather, who told me, "Pat, stop worrying. Do something for me. Look through the book of Psalms. Read it until you find a verse that seems to be speaking to you."

"Psalms? What am I going to find in there?" I asked Heather.

"Just do it. You'll find what you're looking for."

That afternoon I opened my Bible and read the first two psalms. Nothing hit me. The third verse said something about a tree yielding "its fruit in season," which only depressed me more. It made me think of ruby-red grapefruit and large, juicy oranges hanging on trees all over Florida—fruit that I certainly wouldn't be enjoying.

This can't be the verse that's supposed to make me feel better, I thought. I closed the book and opened it again at random. This time, my eyes went directly to Psalms 37:5: "Commit thy way unto the Lord; trust also in Him; and He shall bring it to pass."

Two things about that verse threw me for a loop. The part about committing my way to the Lord—my way to see my son perform in his last game, perhaps? The other was the notion that the Lord would "do this." If I did my part, then God would do His. In other words, if I really, truly trusted in the Lord, then He would bring all things to pass. That was the clincher, since Andrew and I would be flying standby on a "pass."

I thought, "Okay, Patricia, this is it. If Heather can be so dead-bolt certain of her faith, why can't you? You have to put it on the line. Do you truly believe that this is in the hands of the Lord and that He will bring it to pass?"

I only had to ask myself that question once. I sat down that moment and memorized verse 37:5. It was the first Bible verse I'd ever memorized in my life. I've been a longtime Bible reader and student, but memorizing is very difficult for me. I chanted the verse at least a hundred times a day during those weeks before Christmas: "Commit thy way unto the Lord; trust also in Him; and He shall bring it to pass."

The minute I turned the problem over to the Lord, I relaxed completely and virtually sailed through the preparations for Christmas.

Never again did I worry about whether or

not we'd get on the plane, not even when I learned every flight had been greatly oversold with the exception of Christmas morning. And even for that flight, eighty of the eighty-four seats had been sold, with three weeks still to go before Christmas.

For the next three weeks, I repeated my newly memorized verse a thousand times: before I got out of bed in the morning, before each meal, during the day, in the car, in my home office, walking down the hall, in bed at night. I repeated it to all my friends and family and assured them that Andrew and I would be in Tampa for the Hall of Fame Bowl on January 2nd, and that we'd be flying down there on Christmas morning.

Christmas Eve day dawned holy and cold in Milwaukee. Andrew, my grown children, son-in-law, granddaughter, and friends Rusty and Heather and their two little daughters, all celebrated Christ's birth amidst my giggling excitement as I packed our bags for Florida. I shared my memorized Bible verse from Psalms with them as part of the grace before our Christmas Eve dinner.

"So Mom, are you just going to keep going back to the airport every day all week until you get on a plane?" my daughter Julia asked during dessert.

"No, honey, we'll be getting on the plane tomorrow morning. I'll send you postcards and bring you seashells!"

Never before in my life had I been so sure of something—something that to all the sensible people around me seemed to be the folly of the century.

Bags packed, car loaded, Michael drove us to the airport at 7:30 A.M. Christmas Day. The gate agent said there'd been four people with emergencies in Florida, and they'd been given priority standby status.

It didn't matter. I knew that when that gate closed we'd be on the plane.

That afternoon, Andrew and I picked grapefruit from the tree next to the hot tub in the backyard of our friends' house in Florida.

Nine days later, after sunning ourselves on Gulf beaches, exploring exotic wonders and following the Wisconsin marching band as they performed all over Tampa, we watched as the University of Wisconsin defeated Duke in the Hall of Fame Bowl on a beautiful, sunny, eighty-degree day.

Michael's last performance with the band was stellar.

But not quite as stellar as my faith in the Lord—who brings all things to pass.

~Patricia Lorenz
Chicken Soup for the Christian Woman's Soul

The Piano

Coins are round: Sometimes they roll to you,
sometimes to others.
~Folk Saying

During the early 1990s, being a Christian recording artist sometimes felt like one big struggle in a world of extremes. I would stand on stage in front of spotlights and thousands of people, only to go back to the hotel room with my family, wondering if anyone really cared about what I did at all. I would fall into bed in a small room shared by six, with one bathroom and suitcases piled everywhere.

We put on large contemporary Christian concerts in churches all over the country. I

stepped into some of the most beautiful buildings equipped with state of the art furnishings
and accoutrements, only to feel like I was on
the outside looking in. For two hours I was the
center of attention—lights dimmed, music
played and God's presence filled all of our
lives. Then moments after the concert ended,
we packed it all up, rolled it out the back door
into our trailer and disappeared down a lonely
highway into the silence of the night.

I used to walk around those big, empty,
church auditoriums as everyone scurried to
get set up, wondering how they did it. How
did these churches acquire all the wonderful
facilities and resources they needed to make a
difference in people's lives? What was the
secret? I was doing the same thing they were,
only I did it on the road and my "congrega-
tion" changed every night. I wondered how
anyone ever acquired the unabashed boldness
to just stretch their hands open, stand before
God and simply receive from his overflowing
abundance. It was easier to just believe that

everyone else must be doing something right,
and I must be somehow flawed. Maybe if I
tried harder, worked longer and suffered a little bit more, I would finally be "worthy" of
receiving what I needed.

One afternoon between concerts, my husband and I walked into a huge music store
filled with the most impressive collection of
grand pianos I had ever seen. Row after row of
black and ivory concert grands sat there waiting for someone with the gift of music in their
soul to sit down and play them. I pulled a
bench up to one of the pianos, touched the
keys and smiled.

"Nice piano," I said to the salesclerk.

"Are you looking for a grand or a baby grand?"
He perked up, thinking he had a customer.

"Oh me?" I laughed. "Well, I can't really
buy a piano now," I said sheepishly.

My husband walked over and spoke up
without hesitation. "Honey, you've been want-
ing a real piano for years. These are incredible
instruments!"

I gave him the you-are-out-of-your-mind look.

"Let me show you a baby grand over here that's really special," the salesclerk said moving us to the back of the store.

My husband followed him excitedly. I trailed behind, dragging my feet, wishing we could just get out of there and save ourselves any further embarrassment. We didn't belong in an expensive music store. I felt like I was trespassing and any minute I was going to be found out.

"This is a brand-new baby grand," the salesclerk gushed. "It's the only one of its kind, and we're clearing it out. It's on sale—and I'll tell you, it's one of the most fabulous pianos I've ever seen."

"Sit down and play it, " my husband urged.

I wished he'd leave me alone. Why should I play it if I couldn't have it? To save face in front of the salesclerk, I sat down at the clean, white keys. They felt like smooth silk and sounded like a symphony. The salesclerk propped the lid open.

"Press the pedals and play hard," he said. "You can't believe how this thing resonates and fills up the whole room."

He was right. It was incredible. It moved and inspired me to just sit and play it in the store. I could have written a song right then and there.

"How much is it?" my husband asked casually—as if he had just won the lottery.

"It lists for ten thousand dollars, but since we're clearing it out, we're giving it away for only five thousand dollars." He grinned.

"Wow!" my husband cheered and turned smiling at me.

Wow yourself, I thought, rolling my eyes. What did it matter if it was five thousand or five million! We were struggling musicians who didn't have the money. I couldn't have this. I was nobody. We weren't the pastors with the big buildings. We didn't have a record company financing our tours. Who was I to spend that kind of money for a music ministry? Still, I wanted that piano, and my husband knew it.

"Let's put some money down on it and hold it," he whispered to me frantically. "If we can't pay for it in thirty days, then we won't get it, but let's take a step of faith and try."

He handed the salesclerk a check for $500.

The salesclerk smiled. "See you in thirty days!" he said, waving goodbye.

As the days passed, I wanted that piano more than anything. Each day on tour I started my day with prayer time, and from somewhere deep down in my spirit, faith rose. Unabashed boldness seemed to come out of nowhere and I talked to God.

"God, if I were a pastor, and I needed one of those million-dollar buildings to share my message, you would provide it without question. If I was a medical missionary, and the 'tool' I needed was an airplane, it would come to me. Well, God, I'm a musician, and that's a God-given calling as worthy and as important

as any other calling. I'm not asking for a building or an airplane; I'm just asking for a piano
to write my songs. I'm ready to believe that my
gift of music is as important to you as the gift
of being a pastor or a medical missionary or a
brain surgeon. I know you won't fail me
because I'm important, too."

Every morning I prayed that prayer and as
I did, I began to realize that I was just as
"worthy" as anyone else, because God had
given me my musical gift. In a few weeks, I
believed it wholeheartedly and the doubt that
I didn't deserve anything began to fade. I
began to tell my friends about the piano I had
"on hold."

Our concert tour ended twenty-nine days
later. As we pulled into the driveway and
started unloading our gear, my parents, who
had been watching our house, appeared in the
front yard with a letter in their hands.

"Here's the weirdest letter," they said,
handing us the stack of mail. "It's addressed to
you, honey, but your last name is spelled

wrong, and there's no street address. I can't believe it got here."

I stared at the wrinkled, stained envelope with just my name and my small town and state scribbled across it.

I opened it up curiously and saw a yellow check inside. There was no letter or note, just the yellow check. As I unfolded it, I almost fainted. It was for $5,000, and it was made out to me from my great-uncle Britt. I hardly knew him and hadn't spoken to him in many years. My parents looked at the check in shock.

"Honey, what in the world?" my mother gasped.

"My piano," I whispered.

"Uncle Britt did that to me once," my dad laughed. "Sometimes he just likes to start getting rid of all the money he has. I guess your number came up today!" He giggled at his eccentric uncle and hugged me.

The next morning, exactly thirty days later, I called the music store, wired them the full amount of $4,500 and gave the leftover $500 to a worthy ministry. My shiny, white baby grand piano was delivered and placed in the middle of my living room where the sun streamed down on it from a skylight.

There are still times in my life when I feel like "I'm on the outside looking in," and I question whether I'm "worthy" enough. I sometimes wonder if God only blesses big names and big buildings. On those days I sit down in front of the most extravagant concert piano that I have ever played, and I remember that whether anybody else thinks so or not, God believes I am "worth it," and He got a ninety-year-old, eccentric great-uncle to help Him show me.

~Carla Riehl
Chicken Soup for the Christian Woman's Soul

You Can Be Right

What is a friend? A single soul dwelling in two bodies.
~Aristotle

Earl once told his younger sister, Liddy, "If you can hang on my back pocket, you can go anywhere I go, too." So Liddy, six years younger, always tagged along, even on Earl's dates. She once stowed away in the dusty back seat of his truck and popped up when he and his date arrived at the drive-in theater. As Liddy grew into a young beauty, Earl made sure all her suitors met his personal approval.

Even after their marriages, Earl and Liddy remained close. Years later, Liddy's husband, Kirby, when diagnosed with terminal cancer, said, "I won't worry about Liddy as long as Earl is alive."

After Kirby's death, Liddy withdrew from everyone, even Earl. He and his wife, Sue, recognized this as Liddy's way of grieving, but gradually their contact with Liddy diminished. As more time passed, it seemed harder to pick up the phone and call.

One February afternoon, Earl collapsed at work. At the hospital, the doctors told Sue it was a heart attack. They offered what they called a "clot buster" shot to open up the arteries around the heart. The shot worked, and Earl's heart attack lessened. After a successful angioplasty the next morning, the doctors told them, "All is well." Relieved and grateful, Earl and Sue went home to rest and recover.

Within twenty-four hours, Earl's entire body swelled. He returned to the hospital. With sinking hearts, Earl and Sue learned that 1 in 100,000 patients who receive the shot experience a side effect called "cholesterol showering." Instead of breaking up only the clots that caused Earl's heart attack, the medication made all the cholesterol in his body release into his bloodstream. The overload was causing all his organs to slowly shut down. One doctor on the medical team said they would have to amputate one limb at a time to try to save him. "I began wondering how much longer I had to live," says Earl. "Emotionally, Sue and I hit bottom. We were both so scared, we didn't know how to comfort each other."

At home a few days later, Sue and Earl received a special phone call. It was Earl's sister Liddy. "I heard about Earl.... I wish I knew what to do. If only Kirby were here...." Liddy's voice broke with little sobs. "May I come over to see you? I'd understand if you said no.... Would you ask Earl?"

Sue gently replied, "I don't need to. We both want to see you—as soon as you can get here." Liddy surprised Earl and Sue by arriving at their home with all her children and grandchildren. Sue hugged each one as Earl watched from the couch where he lay. When

Liddy greeted him she said, "It's been a long time, brother." Earl replied, "Give me a hug!" Receiving his hug, he whispered to her, "Can we put lost time behind us?"

"I'd like that," Liddy responded softly, tears brimming over her eyelids and streaming down her cheeks. She sat on the footstool beside him. "Can you forgive me for staying away for so long?"

"You know I can, Sis. I just want us to be brother and sister again, especially now," Earl said, reaching out his hand to wipe away her tears. Liddy grasped Earl's muscular, yet swollen hand and simply said, "I sure missed you."

In the following days, Earl's spirits were up. Not able to leave the house, he had time to rethink what was really important to him. "I realized that if I was going to die, I didn't want anyone I left behind to be angry with me," he says. He began calling friends and cousins he had not seen for years. Some had drifted out of his life for no particular reason. Others, though, carried grudges or hurt feelings. One man, for example, had not talked to Earl for twenty years because of a misunderstanding. Earl called him on the telephone and said, "I don't remember what we disagreed about, but whatever it was, you can be right. I don't want there to be any negative feelings between us." Every person he called came to visit him. One woman, suffering from severe physical pain of her own, came in a wheelchair to visit him during one of his hospital stays.

After many trips to the local hospital for tests and treatment, with only a medical file as thick as a phone book to show for it, Earl and Sue decided to travel to a nearby city to discuss Earl's case with a renowned kidney specialist. The specialist gave Earl a month to live.

Soon after, Earl's niece Ronda, one of Liddy's daughters who worked in the medical field, asked another famous kidney specialist his opinion of what her uncle was going through. This doctor offered a glimmer of hope. He instructed, "Tell your uncle to go to bed; it may take two years, but total rest might allow the cholesterol to filter out of his system naturally." Having exhausted all other options, or so it seemed, Earl agreed to stay in bed for as long as it would take.

Though they had no one to talk to who had survived this rare "cholesterol showering," Earl and Sue found comfort in the renewed friendships that Earl had initiated. Phone calls of support came daily. And since medicine offered no answers, everyone they knew agreed to pray.

Late one night, after months of resting and waiting, Sue begged Earl to try something new. She told him, "We've prayed for your health many times, but I've noticed that the Bible also talks about anointing sick people with oil and asking others to pray over them. Could we at least try?" She nervously awaited his answer, knowing that the Earl she knew before this ordeal would have never agreed. But, she hoped that with all he'd been through, he might be willing.

Sue was not disappointed. With Earl's approval, she called the minister at their church and asked him to come and anoint Earl with oil and pray for him. Though it was nearly 3:00 A.M., the minister and a deacon arrived, ready to do as Sue asked.

The next evening, the entire deacon board came. The members gathered around the bed where Earl was confined, and each took a turn praying. After everyone left, Earl and Sue knelt by their respective sides of the bed to continue praying.

On his knees, Earl realized, "What am I doing out of bed? I'm better!" His arms and legs no longer ached, and the swelling was gone. "When it dawned on us what had happened," Earl says, "we got so excited, we went into our backyard in our pajamas and danced together under the stars!

"I knew in my heart that I had a lot to celebrate: first, all my friends, and now, my health, too!"

Several years later, Earl, now in his late

sixties, is in excellent health. More important, though, he says, "Facing death, I realized more than ever how deeply I care for my friends. And I no longer need to be 'right.' Standing by what I believe will always be important, but it doesn't mean I have to insist that everyone agree with me.

"Reaching out, forgiving and telling others, 'Look, you can be right,' didn't cost me a thing. It gained for me one of the greatest treasures this life offers: old friendships. And I got back my sister, too."

Now Earl and Sue talk to Liddy nearly every day. She is hanging on his back pocket again after all these years.

~Amy Seeger
Chicken Soup for the Golden Soul

Life, What a Beautiful Gift

You don't choose your family. They are God's gift
to you, as you are to them.
~Desmond Tutu

It was the first week in December. My daughter Julie and I had decided to go Christmas shopping. We have always been extra close, and I always looked forward to this special time together. We would do some "serious" shopping, go out for lunch, and catch up on what was happening in each other's lives.

Over lunch, we discussed what gifts we would buy our relatives and friends. I always felt this was a real chore, as I was always worried about treating all five of my children equally, finding something they didn't already have. Julie, on the other hand, is a person who always seems to find the perfect gift for everyone. Everything has to be the perfect color, the perfect size, the perfect scent! She goes back and forth, from store to store, to get the best bargain.

That day, while eating, our conversation somehow switched from Christmas gifts to life's blessings. This made both of us think of my illness. Although I had been extremely sick several times, for the most part, I still considered myself truly blessed. In fact there had been several times when my M.S. or lupus were out of remission, and my doctor said it was indeed a miracle that I was still alive. Maybe it was a miracle, or maybe God just had other plans for me.

Realizing how lucky I was, when Julie asked me what I wanted for Christmas, I tried to tell her without ruining her Christmas spirit, that I didn't expect or even want a present. I explained just getting together with my beautiful family was all I could hope for.

Julie looked disappointed in my reply. "Oh, Mom," she said, "you are always so darn practical! There has to be something little you want."

I repeated what I had said, "I have a fantastic husband, beautiful children, and now two beautiful granddaughters. I have it all! What more could anyone want in one life?" I was speaking with my entire heart. I truly felt that way. I loved my family so much that little else was important. Each day I thanked God for giving me yet one more twenty-four hours to share with them.

Suddenly, without even thinking, I added, "I know this is selfish, but you know, I really would love to have a grandson before I die! Now that would be neat!"

Julie just shook her head, and said, "I give up!"

"Well, you asked what I would like, didn't you? I have always wanted a grandson! I love little boys! I'll never forget how happy I was to have your brother after all you girls! Oh, I love all of you equally, that is for certain, but there is something very special about little boys! Now if you can find a way to get me a grandson before Christmas, I will take him and love him without complaining!"

"You're impossible!" Julie added. "Let's finish our shopping. You won't accept a little gift, yet you ask for the world! Mothers!"

Hours later, Julie dropped me off at my house. Exhausted from shopping, I hugged her and promised to let her know if I thought of anything "easier" for her to get for me.

When I went in the house, the first thing I did was check our new answering machine for messages. The blinking red light indicated there were several.

The first message was another daughter whose voice assured me that she was concerned because I had gone away for that long without first obtaining permission! I thought it was ironic remembering the times my children had forgotten to call me when they were going to be late. Funny how time changes roles. The second message was to remind me of an upcoming craft auction at church, and the third to confirm a dental appointment. Who needed to be reminded of such things? I started to walk out of the room, when I heard the last voice, that of my husband. He sounded more than a little confused.

"Barb! Are you home? If you are home, then pick this thing up! Can't you hear me? I need to talk to you... Q-U-I-C-K!" Frustrated, when at last he realized he was talking to an electronic piece of equipment, he lowered his voice and said, "Please, Honey, when you get home... CALL ME!"

Wow! This was so unlike the cool man I was used to! What could be wrong? I knew I had to call him back at once.

Call I did. It was not only a shocking call, but also an unplanned answer to a prayer, and that something little I had wanted for my Christmas gift. About the same time I was telling Julie that I would like a grandson before my life was finished, a young girl in a nearby

town had called my husband at work to tell
him that she was the mother of a little grandson we had never met! We were both in shock.
This woman explained she had a brief relationship with our son, had gotten pregnant, and
had a little boy who was now seven months
old! She said she had pleaded with our son to
tell us about the baby. However, he was afraid
we would be disappointed in him if we knew,
so he had made her promise not to tell.

For some unknown reason that day, she
had decided that it was unfair to us to keep
this grandchild a secret any longer. Since our
home number was unlisted, she had called the
place my husband worked and told him the
story.

My husband gave me the woman's number, and said she had told him I was free to
make arrangements to meet our little grandson
if I liked. Grandson! Liked? I was a doubting
Thomas. I had to see for myself. I called the
woman, and within an hour, I was on the way
to see this baby. If she was telling the truth I

had a grandson! No matter how complicated the details of his conception were, I knew I would love him. I was happy, sad, excited and tearful all at the same time.

When I arrived at the given address, I was met at the door by the woman and her other children. I sensed all of them were trying to evaluate me, and this made me feel terribly uncomfortable. My first impulse was to turn and run. Something within me told me I had to stay. I offered her my hand; she took it. She invited me inside. Walking ahead of me to a nearby table, she picked up an envelope and handed it to me. "Here are the paternity papers," she said. "Here's proof that Toby is your grandson!"

I had just learned something else: Her baby's name was Toby. I questioned the baby's last name, and I was told he had received my son's last name the previous day in court.

Nearly collapsing, I lowered myself to the nearest chair. I didn't realize the girl had left the room until I saw her return, carrying a little boy. She walked up to me, placed the most beautiful little baby into my arms, and said, "Son, I think it is time you meet your grandma!" Toby looked right up at me and gave me the biggest smile... I cried.

At that moment, little Toby became a very important part of my life. My son and the baby's mother had made a big mistake. However, God himself had created little Toby, and God doesn't make mistakes. I had a grandson! A beautiful bundle of joy! What a precious Christmas gift!

Later that evening, my husband and I had a long talk with our son. We told him we knew about Toby, and I was hurt that he could even think for a moment that his father and I could have loved him less for having made a mistake. I told him if we only love our children when they live their lives the way we feel they should, then that isn't really love. He told me that when Toby's mother first discovered she was pregnant, she had considered an abortion, and we cried together, thanking God she hadn't. Later, we even laughed a little over the speedy way in which God seemed to answer my Christmas gift request!

Since then many Christmases have passed. Toby spends a lot of time with his father and with us, as well. Every day, but especially on Christmas, I am so thankful for this very special gift I received eight years ago.

~Barbara Jeanne Fisher
Chicken Soup for the Grandparent's Soul

Miracle Wallet

*Our deeds determine us, as much
as we determine our deeds.*
~George Eliot

As a military wife of sixteen years, I stay quite busy and have little time for reflection. As a mother of three children and a nurse with a small teaching job, you can guess I don't often think about times past. Over the years, we have traveled and lived in many different places, and there have been many people who have touched our lives in ways that I will never forget. Despite hectic schedules, sometimes a story needs to be shared with others.

We were stationed at Fort Campbell outside

of Clarksville, Tennessee, only three hours away from our hometown of Florence, Alabama. My husband was on temporary duty in Africa, and I thought I would take my two girls home for a few days to give them some time with their grandparents. I needed a break, and four-year-old Bethany and ten-year-old Sydney would enjoy the trip.

One crisp, clear spring morning, we set out for home in our small station wagon. After an hour on the road, I pulled off the interstate at Brentwood and stopped at a gas station. A while later, I needed to stop again to buy some snacks for the girls. I reached for my wallet to get change... and it was gone. No!

I thought about the gas station where I had stopped earlier. Okay, I thought, trying to calm myself in front of the children, think! Into the station... bought juice after the bathroom... then out to the car... strapped Bethany in... The wallet! I put it on top of the car beside the luggage rack! Oh no! I already knew the answer but stole a quick look at the top of the car to confirm it wasn't still there.

I did a quick mental inventory. As a military dependent, my identification card was vital to my survival in everyday life, especially with my husband gone. Also, my Social Security card, driver's license and my adopted daughter's green card were in there! I couldn't easily replace that! It was the longest drive to Florence, and I reluctantly told my in-laws about the wallet I left on top of my car.

My father-in-law and I hurried to call the Brentwood police. They hadn't heard of anyone turning in my wallet but promised to look around the gas station and ask the attendants there if anyone had turned it in.

I knew in my mind that there was little to no possibility of my wallet being found, much less returned to me, as I had no current address or phone numbers in it, thanks to our many military moves.

The next day, the phone rang. The girl said she was calling from the Blockbuster Video in Florence. She asked my name and if

I had a Blockbuster card in my wallet.

"Yes," I answered, very puzzled.

"Someone has found your wallet and is waiting here at our store. Can you come? They'll be outside waiting for you."

"Of course! I'll be right there!" I scrambled out the door, totally confused, amazed and happy. As I pulled up into the parking lot, I saw a station wagon with three people sitting in the back with the hatch up, two women and a man. I stepped out of the car, and the younger lady came up to me and asked, "Are you Lisa?"

It seems the couple and her mother were on a day trip from Tennessee to the Dismals, a nature park in northwest Alabama. As her mom said, "I have this bad smokin' habit, and I guess the good Lord's tryin' to tell me somethin' 'cause I caught myself on fire as we pulled the car back onto the interstate from Brentwood. I pulled over to jump out and brush off the ashes, and as I was walking behind the car I saw your wallet."

At this point she scolded me. "Honey, you need to promise me to put your address and phone number in your wallet 'cause we couldn't find anything but that Blockbuster card to possibly help us find you!"

This family went out of their way to find the Blockbuster Video with the hope of the store being able to find me. I hadn't used that card, having gotten it in Florence on a previous visit, but the account had a phone number! Luckily for me, the most logical route from Tennessee to the Dismals goes right through... Florence, Alabama.

Of course, I thanked them profusely, but I still regret that I never thought to get their address. That kind act reminded me that there are truly honest people in our world, no matter how bleak things seem when we read the newspaper.

So, to that certain family of three, you seemed more like angels to me. If you are reading this story, I thank you again for your honesty, caring and kindness.

And to the mom in the group: my phone number and address are now in my wallet, updated with every move!

~Lisa Cobb
Chicken Soup for the Military Wife's Soul

In Better Hands

Prayer is the universal language.
~Author Unknown

On the way home from the small Himalayan kingdom of Bhutan, I met with Mother Teresa. Not once but twice.

My friend Laurie and I had flown into Calcutta from Paro in the early afternoon. We had one day in the City of Joy before she would fly on to Bangkok and I would return to Canada via New Delhi, Bombay, and a brief stay with my father in London.

Over lunch, we toyed with the notion of visiting Mother Teresa's orphanage. A taxi ride and a couple of hours later, we were touched by the sight of forty to fifty little kids playing in a small courtyard, half of them running around completely undressed, the others in blue and white striped outfits. As we were leaving, a sister informed us that Mother Teresa's residence was in a building called Mother House, only a few blocks away.

Within minutes we were standing in front of a rather inconspicuous wooden door with a large cross on it. On a small wooden sign to the left of the door, in white lettering, were the modest words, MOTHER TERESA. When asked who we wished to see, we answered simply and in unison, "Mother Teresa." The sister showed us in and, in a short while, informed us that Mother Teresa would meet with us.

We found ourselves waiting nervously on an old bench, trying to figure out what we were going to say. Suddenly, from behind two swinging doors, we saw a white-and-blue sari and two bare feet in open sandals. We gazed in awe as Mother Teresa moved briskly toward us. She sat next to Laurie, took her hand, and got right down to business.

She asked us where we were from and whether we were volunteers. She described the trip she had just taken to Montreal. She told us that she was in a hurry as she was leaving again the next day. With that, she got up, disappeared behind a screen partition and quickly returned with two cards bearing her picture and a small prayer. She signed both: "God bless you. Teresa M.C." and left. Though neither of us was particularly religious, we just sat there, frozen in a state of reverence.

The next day Laurie left for Bangkok and I left for London. Checking in at the Air India counter in Delhi, I couldn't help but hear a woman with jet black hair draped in flowing Indian fabrics shouting at the next counter. In her distinctly Greek accent, she was raging about not getting a particular bulkhead seat. Within seconds, boarding pass in hand, she brazenly marched away from the scene and through the terminal.

A few hours later, when it came time to board, I started towards the gate. As I approached security control, out of the corner of my eye I noticed a pair of sandals and a blue-and-white sari. I looked over and saw a sister of the Missionaries of Charity. And then another. And another—a gaggle of sisters scurrying straight through security. At the very end raced Mother Teresa, carrying nothing but a single book—her Bible. In a glance, she was out of sight.

At the gate, I looked around for a place to sit and spotted the Greek woman, anxiously staring at the departure board. I sat down, and sure enough, she sat right next to me.

We started talking and, when I mentioned meeting Mother Teresa, her mouth dropped. She reached for a cross around her neck and told me how much she had always wanted to meet Mother Teresa. I recounted how I had seen Mother Teresa again only minutes before. My Greek gate-mate struck my arm in disbelief. Oh, how she wanted the chance to meet this living saint!

When we arrived in the Bombay terminal, they told us that our connecting plane was going to be delayed for a "few hours."

Thirty or forty very irate Italian tourists were grabbing their heads, motioning madly with their hands, and screaming at the poor airline attendants and each other. I wandered away from the chaos in search of a place to sleep.

I finally found one of those horrible plastic airport chairs on the other side of the airport, and using my daypack as a pillow, I fell fast asleep.

A couple of hours later, I felt a hand nudge me. Startled, I looked up. It was the Greek woman.

She wanted me to go with her, to follow her. She was very forceful and determined. She explained that Mother Teresa wanted to see me. Of course, I had no idea what this woman was talking about but, after more pleading, I went along. After all, what else did I have to do at four o'clock in the morning?

We got to the door of the business and first-class lounge. She mumbled to the guard that I was with her, and I followed behind.

The room was small and dark. All ten people were sprawled about on couches, fast asleep. The Greek woman motioned to the far corner near a dim light. Sitting there in a hard chair, hunched over, was Mother Teresa, reading. While every other much younger, mortal soul was sleeping, she was wide awake, praying in the middle of the night.

Whispering, the Greek woman prodded me, "You must go and talk to her."

"I can't, she's praying," I replied.

"Just go now!"

"I can't, not until she's finished," I insisted.

We sat down, gazing as she prayed, noting her every movement.

My Hellenic messenger introduced herself as Jenny and related in a soft voice how she and Mother Teresa had talked for a short while earlier on. This was not the same crazy woman whom I had first encountered at the check-in counter in Delhi. She carefully and proudly showed me the necklace of the Virgin Mary that Mother Teresa had given her. She rubbed it and continued.

"She's been praying the whole time," she said, shaking her head in reverent disbelief.

Suddenly, Mother Teresa placed the prayer book down on her lap.

"Go over now!" the Greek woman beseeched.

I got up and inched my way towards the light.

"Mother Teresa, I'm sorry to disturb you but we met yesterday in Calcutta at Mother House."

Her wrinkled face strained upwards to meet my puzzled eyes. "God works in mysterious ways," she quipped. She invited me to sit next to her.

As I sat down, I couldn't wait to ask her about the serendipitous nature of our two meetings. "What does this mean, meeting you again? Is there something I should be doing?"

"What are you doing?" she asked.

"Traveling," I replied impulsively.

She took my hand. "You must look for the truth, and guide others to look for the truth. Time is short. There is so much to do and so little time. You will know what to do."

We talked for an hour, mostly about her missions around the world, before she excused herself to return to her prayers. I withdrew and sat next to Jenny. Together, we studied this winner of the Nobel Prize in the peace of her prayers.

Just after seven o'clock, we heard our flight being called for boarding. As we got up, so did Mother Teresa. She was on our flight.

As soon as the plane took off, I fell asleep. A few hours later, I awoke and went to freshen up.

Leaving the toilet cabin, I heard commotion from the section ahead. I turned the corner, looked up the aisle toward the front of the plane, and glimpsed Mother Teresa's blue-and-white sari just as she was returning to the first-class section. In the brief time that I was in the restroom, she had gone through the whole plane and blessed all of its passengers.

In her wake, the large group of Italians, who only hours before were wound up in a frenzied state of frustration and anger, were now crying and praying, and very, very grateful. Many were down on their knees making the sign of the cross, while others couldn't stop hugging and kissing one another.

Men and women queued from the left side of the plane into a makeshift first-class confessional, emerging moments later on the other side into the embrace of their fellow countrymen and passengers.

The plane stopped in Rome, where the Italians and Mother Teresa deplaned. I read the next day that she had an audience with the Pope.

On my arrival at Heathrow, my father met me, his face ashen. He recounted the morning's news: A plane had crashed in Bombay, around the same time that mine had taken off. He was terrified that somehow I was on that ill-fated flight.

"Well, Dad," I began my story, "if I were, I couldn't have been in better hands."

~Steve Zikman
Chicken Soup for the Traveler's Soul

The Four Chaplains

For this is God. Our God forever and ever.
He will be our guide.
~Psalm 48:14

In November 1942, four men met while attending Chaplain's School at Harvard University. At age forty-two, George Fox was the eldest. The youngest was thirty-year-old Clark Poling, and the other two, Alexander Goode and John Washington, were both thirty-two.

Reverend Fox, from Vermont, enlisted in the Army the same day his eighteen-year-old son Wyatt enlisted in the Marine Corps. During World War I, Fox—then only seventeen years old—had convinced the Army he was actually eighteen and enlisted as a medical corps assistant. His courage on the battlefield earned him the Silver Star, the Croix de Guerre and the Purple Heart. When World War II broke out, he told his family, "I've got to go. I know from experience what our boys are about to face. They need me."

Reverend Poling was from Ohio and pastoring in New York when World War II began. He determined to enter the Army, but not as a chaplain. He didn't want to hide behind the church, "in some safe office out of the firing line," he told his father.

But his father, Reverend Daniel Poling, knew something of war, having served as a chaplain himself during World War I. He told his son, "Don't you know that chaplains have the highest mortality rate of all? As a chaplain, you can't carry a gun." With new appreciation for the role of the Chaplains Corps, Clark Poling accepted a commission.

Alexander Goode's father was a clergyman, too. While studying to follow in his father's footsteps, Alex had joined the National Guard. When war was declared, he wanted to become a chaplain. He chose to do so as a U.S. Army chaplain.

Mild-mannered John P. Washington left one with the impression that he was not the sort of man to go to war and become a hero. His love of music and beautiful voice belied the toughness inside. As one of nine children in an Irish immigrant family living in the toughest part of Newark, New Jersey, he had learned through sheer determination to hold his own in any fight. Like the others, he wanted to serve wherever his country needed him.

Upon meeting at the chaplains' school, the four men quickly became friends. What makes this fact remarkable is the enormous differences in their backgrounds: Reverend Fox was a Methodist minister, Reverend Poling was a Dutch Reformed minister, Father Washington was a Catholic priest and Goode was a Jewish rabbi.

After graduating from Harvard, the friends

were assigned to posts in Europe. The four chaplains said goodbye to their families and reported to New York to board the transport that would take them overseas.

The Dorchester was an aging, luxury coastal liner that was no longer luxurious. Pressed into service as a transport ship, all noncritical amenities had been removed and cots were crammed into every available space. The intent was to get as many young fighting men as possible on each voyage.

When the soldiers boarded on January 23, 1943, the Dorchester was filled to capacity. In addition to the Merchant Marine crew and a few civilians, young soldiers filled every available space. There were 902 lives about to be cast to the mercy of the frigid North Atlantic.

As the Dorchester left New York for an Army base in Greenland, many dangers lay ahead. The sea itself was always dangerous, especially in this area known for ice flows, raging waters and gale-force winds. The greatest danger, however, was the ever-present threat

of German submarines, which had recently
been sinking Allied ships at the rate of one
hundred every month. The Dorchester would
be sailing through an area that had become
infamous as "Torpedo Junction."

Most of the men who boarded for the trip
were young, frightened soldiers. Many were
going to sea for the first time and suffered sea-
sickness for days. They were packed head to
toe below deck, a human sea of fear and uncer-
tainty. Even if they survived the eventual
Atlantic crossing, they didn't have much to
look forward to, only the prospects of being
thrown into the cauldron of war on foreign
shores. They were men in need of a strong
shoulder to lean on, a firm voice to encourage
them and a ray of hope in a world at war. In
their midst moved the four Army chaplains:
Fox, Goode, Poling and Washington.

The crossing was filled with long hours of
boredom and discomfort. Outside, the chilly
Arctic winds and cold ocean spray coated the
Dorchester's deck with ice. Below deck, the

soldiers' quarters were hot from too many bodies, crammed into too small a place for too many days in a row.

Finally, on February 2nd, the Dorchester was within 150 miles of Greenland. It would have generated a great sense of relief among the young soldiers crowded in the ship's berths, had not the welcome news been tempered by other more ominous news. One of the Dorchester's three Coast Guard escorts had received sonar readings during the day, indicating the presence of an enemy submarine in "Torpedo Junction."

The Dorchester's captain listened to the news with great concern. If he could make it through the night, air cover would arrive with daylight to safely guide his ship home. The problem would be surviving the night. Aware of the potential for disaster, he instructed the soldiers to sleep in their clothes and life jackets... just in case.

Outside it was another cold, windy night as the midnight hour signaled the passing of

February 2nd and the beginning of a new day. In the distance a cold, metal arm broke the surface of the stormy seas. At the end of that arm, a German U-Boat (submarine) captain monitored the slowly passing troop transport. Shortly before one in the morning, he gave the command to fire.

Quiet moments passed as the torpedo silently streaked toward the Dorchester. Then the early morning was shattered by the flash of a blinding explosion and the roar of massive destruction. The "hit" had been dead on, tossing men from their cots with the force of its explosion. A second torpedo followed the first, instantly killing one hundred men in the hull of the ship.

Power was knocked out by the explosion in the engine room, and darkness engulfed the frightened men below deck as water rushed through gaping wounds in the Dorchester's hull. The ship tilted at an unnatural angle as it began to sink rapidly. Wounded men cried out in pain, frightened survivors screamed in terror and all groped frantically in the darkness for exits they couldn't find.

In the darkness, four voices of calm began to speak words of comfort, seeking to bring order to panic and bedlam. Slowly, soldiers began to find their way to the deck of the ship, where they were confronted by the cold winds blowing down from the Arctic. One soldier, reeling from the cold, headed back towards his cabin.

"Where are you going?" a voice asked.

"To get my gloves," the soldier replied.

"Here, take these," said Rabbi Goode as he handed a pair of gloves to the young officer, who would never have survived the trip to his cabin and then back to safety.

"I can't take your gloves," the soldier replied.

"Never mind," the rabbi responded. "I have two pairs."

The young soldier slipped the gloves over his hands and returned to the frigid deck, never stopping to ponder until later when he had reached safety that there was no way Rabbi Goode would have been carrying a spare set of gloves.

Elsewhere on the ship, Reverend Poling guided the frightened soldiers to the deck, their only hope of safety on the rapidly sinking transport. As he led the men, he spoke quietly but firmly, urging them not to give up.

Meanwhile, Reverend Fox and Father Washington tended to the wounded and dying soldiers. Somehow, by their combined efforts, the chaplains succeeded in getting many of the soldiers out of the hold and onto the Dorchester's slippery deck.

In the chaos around them, lifeboats floated away before men could board them. Others capsized as panicked soldiers loaded the small craft beyond limit. The strength, calm and organization of the chaplains, so critical in the dark hull, were still urgently needed. Taking charge, they organized the lifeboat boarding, directed men to safety and left them with parting words of encouragement.

In little more than twenty minutes, the Dorchester was almost gone. Icy waves broke over the railing, tossing men into the sea, many of them without life jackets. In the last moments of the transport's existence, the chaplains were too occupied opening lockers to pass out life jackets to note the threat to their own lives.

Now water was beginning to flow across the deck of the sinking Dorchester. Working against time, the chaplains continued to pass out the life vests from the lockers as the soldiers pressed forward in a ragged line. And then the lockers were all empty, the life jackets gone.

Those still pressing in line began to realize they were doomed; there was no hope. And then something amazing happened, something those who were there would never forget. All four chaplains began taking their own life jackets off and putting them on the men around them.

Then time ran out. The chaplains had done

all they could for those who would survive, and nothing more could be done for the others... including themselves.

Those who had been fortunate enough to reach lifeboats struggled to distance themselves from the sinking ship, to avoid being pulled down by the chasm created as the transport slipped under the surface. Then, amid the sounds of fear and pain that permeated the cold dark night, they heard the strong voices of the chaplains.

"Shma Yisroel Adonai Elohenu Adonai Echod."

"Our Father, which art in Heaven, Hallowed be Thy name. Thy kingdom come, Thy will be done...."

Looking back, the men in the lifeboats could see the slanting deck of the Dorchester, its demise almost complete. Four figures were clearly visible as they stood braced against the railings, praying, singing and giving strength to others by their final valiant declaration of faith. Reverend Fox, Rabbi Goode, Reverend

Poling and Father Washington linked their arms together and leaned into each other for support.

Then, only twenty-seven minutes after the first torpedo struck, the last trace of the Dorchester disappeared beneath the cold North Atlantic waters, taking with it many men, including the four chaplains of different faiths who had found strength in their diversity by focusing on the love for God—and mankind—they all shared.

~The Chapel of Four Chaplains
Chicken Soup for the Veteran's Soul

The Miracle
of Medjugorje

To the immigrant who comes on dreams
and bears the mirror that reflects us all.
Keep faith—this place is capable of miracles.
~Lindalee Tracey, A Scattering of Seeds

Mom always had a great devotion to the
Virgin Mary. She didn't believe that Mary
could answer prayers, but that she was an
intercessor to her son, Jesus. While my mom
was raising eight kids, she likely thought she
needed all the interceding she could get!

Each of us had a rosary, and my mother
taught us to say the Hail Mary on each bead.

make these with her daughters. They were only four, five and eight when she died. Mamma G's Meatloaf was a recipe passed down from Zeke's mother. I imagine Jennifer as a young bride mixing together the pork, beef and veal with sage, parsley and eggs to make her husband's favorite dinner in the hope it would please him. I have made the same meatloaf (as a not-so-young bride) with the same hope in mind.

And here's a collection of recipes printed off the Internet from The Barefoot Contessa, which promise "scrumptious party platters sure to sate even the most grinch-hearted guest" for the holidays. The five pages are stapled together and include recipes for Sun Dried Tomato Dip and Grilled Lemon Chicken with Satay Sauce. I look at the date it was printed—11/30/00. This was a year after she was diagnosed with cancer, two years before she died. "So," I think, "she was still planning on having dinner parties and entertaining." In the face of chemo and cancer, I admire her so I can ask for a miracle," she added emphatically.

But many who went, did. There were hundreds of accounts of miraculous healings and faith conversions at Medjugorje.

Her tour group arrived in Medjugorje late one damp November night. The next morning, they learned their scheduled trek had been postponed, due to the rain and slippery slopes. One younger man who had made the trip twice before, said he could wait no longer—he was climbing the mile-long mountain path right then. My mother said, "Me, too."

So with a pin in her ankle, five metal rods in her back and a song in her heart, my mom set off for the climb. She was surprised to see the trail was only jagged rocks. Step by cautious step, she hiked upward—past a woman even older than she, kneeling in prayerful meditation, and past a half-dozen rowdy ten-year-old boys, running and yelping with joy. Soon they raced ahead of her and later she came upon them again, kneeling in quiet prayer.

Within two hours, my mother stood in wonder and awe at the top of the mountain, on the very site the Virgin had appeared. She knelt in the sprinkling rain and did what she always did—she prayed for her children.

The trek down was even more difficult than the ascent. Each step on the rugged rocks jarred her as she struggled to find stable footing. The rain intensified as they wound their way through the foreign streets. Mom returned to the group, soaking wet but marveling that, not only had she made the climb, she had done so without her usual pain. "Maybe that was the miracle," she mused.

The next day was just another day in wartorn Bosnia, but it was Thanksgiving Day in the States—and the tour guide had a plan to make it a day of thanksgiving in Medjugorje, too. On every tour, the staff purchased and distributed groceries and supplies to the most needy in the community. All of the dozen members of my mother's tour group readily

My Father's Famous Tuna Melt

Sometimes the poorest man leaves
his children the richest inheritance.
~Ruth E. Renkel

I can still remember the smell of hot tuna fresh out of the oven. I could be all the way up in my bedroom on the third floor of our old Victorian-style house and the odor would snake its way around corners, up three flights of stairs and to my bed where it would hover over me, jolting me from a sound sleep. I would be nauseated, on the verge of retching, covering my face with my pillow, but I just couldn't escape the fact that my father was making one of his famous, much-beloved tuna melts. Fresh white albacore with just the right amount of mayo, topped with an expertly browned piece of melted cheddar on a slice of toasted seeded rye. It was simple, but according to experts, it was perfection.

My father was as proud of his culinary creation as he was of his son winning a Little League trophy. His tuna melt was legendary. Friends and neighbors found any excuse to drop by on the off chance he would offer to make them one. And of course, he would rarely disappoint their eager palates. Everyone loved my father's tuna melt. That is, everyone but me.

The truth is, I never tried one. Not even a bite. I was just a kid and my taste buds demanded the simpler things in life—pizza, burgers, hot dogs. They were not sophisticated or daring enough to take a chance on hot fish covered in cheese.

My father pleaded with me through the years to give it a try. "Trust me," he would say, "you'll love it. Have I ever let you down before?" Truth is, he hadn't. His love guided me through my childhood, making sure I never had to worry about a thing. He taught with sorrow. "We have other families waiting for these—we promised them."

The team sat, despondent, until the driver stopped at yet another war-damaged home. A couple who looked years older than my mom were caring for two grown sons, each suffering from a wasting muscular disease. Yet their faith and joy exceeded even that of the team as they crowded the entire group into their tiny kitchen to pray—then insisted that they all share in the food the old woman had prepared for them.

And so went the day, house after house, family after family, each physically destitute and spiritually wealthy.

"That's twenty-four!" the guide said as she checked the last name off the list after the final stop.

"No, twenty-three," someone corrected. "There is one bag of food left."

Dumbfounded, the group looked in the back of the bus to see one lone bag of food.

"We all counted the bags and the people on

the list three times," one member said breathlessly.

"There was no error," the guide said. Then, smiling, she asked, "Are there loaves and fish in that bag?"

The entire team stared at each other—first in confusion, then in awe, then in elation. They cheered, "Let's go!"

The bus returned to the ramshackle house at the end of the lane, and the man and two boys raced out, as if they were expecting them.

~LeAnn Thieman
Chicken Soup for the Christian Woman's Soul

of the room before he even had a chance to remove it from the oven. And before I was able to see the look of disappointment on his face. That was the last tuna melt he ever made before he got sick.

As the cancer took its toll on his body, my father lost his appetite. As great as his will was, he could no longer do many of the things he loved: playing catch in the backyard, helping me with schoolwork, cooking. And he lost his ability to go through the painstaking steps necessary to create his tuna melt. Anything less than perfection would not be accepted. And surely the smell of hot tuna would not sit very well with him anymore.

What pained him more than not being able to eat his beloved tuna melts was not being able to make them for others and share in their joy and pleasure. Now neighbors and friends stopped by for a different reason.

My father had lost a lot of weight along with his appetite and could no longer leave his bed. I spent many nights lying next to him as

Andrew, my thirteen-year-old, and I drove across two states to meet Jan Turner.

Andrew dozed most of the way during the long drive, but every once in a while I'd start a conversation.

"She's handicapped, you know."

"So what's wrong with her? Does she have a disease?"

"I don't think so. But for some reason, she had to have both arms and legs amputated."

"Wow. How does she get around?"

"I'm not sure. We'll see when we get there."

"Does she have any kids?"

"Two boys—Tyler and Cody—both adopted. She's a single parent, too. Only she's never been married."

"So what happened to her?"

"Four years ago Jan was just like me, a busy single mother. She was a full-time music teacher at a grade school and taught all sorts of musical instruments. She was also the music director at her church."

Andrew fell asleep again before I could

finish telling him what little I did know about what had happened to Jan. As I drove across Minnesota, I began to wonder how the woman I was about to meet could cope with such devastating news that all four limbs had to be amputated. How did she learn to survive? Did she have live-in help?

When we arrived in Willmar, Minnesota, I called Jan from our hotel to tell her that I could come to her house and pick her and the boys up, so they could swim at our hotel while we talked.

"That's okay, Pat, I can drive. The boys and I will be there in ten minutes. Would you like to go out to eat first? There's a Ponderosa close to your hotel."

"Sure, that'll be fine," I said haltingly, wondering what it would be like to eat in a public restaurant with a woman who had no arms or legs. And how on earth would she drive? Ten minutes later, Jan pulled up in front of the hotel. She got out of the car, walked over to me with perfect posture on legs and feet that looked every bit as real as mine, and extended her right arm with its shiny hook on the end to shake my hand. "Hello, Pat, I'm sure glad to meet you. And this must be Andrew."

I grabbed her hook, pumped it a bit and smiled sheepishly. "Uh, yes, this is Andrew." I looked in the back seat of her car and smiled at the two boys who grinned back. Cody, the younger one, was practically effervescent at the thought of going swimming in the hotel pool after dinner.

Jan bubbled as she slid back behind the driver's seat, "So hop in. Cody, move over and make room for Andrew."

We arrived at the restaurant, went through the line, paid for our food, and ate and talked amidst the chattering of our three sons. The only thing I had to do for Jan Turner that entire evening was unscrew the top on the ketchup bottle.

Later that night, as our three sons splashed in the pool, Jan and I sat on the side and she told me about life before her illness.

"We were a typical single-parent family. You know, busy all the time. Life was so good, in fact, that I was seriously thinking about adopting a third child."

My conscience stung. I had to face it—the woman next to me was better at single parenting than I ever thought about being.

Jan continued. "One Sunday in November of 1989, I was playing my trumpet at the front of my church when I suddenly felt weak, dizzy and nauseous. I struggled down the aisle, motioned for the boys to follow me and drove home. I crawled into bed, but by evening I knew I had to get help."

Jan then explained that by the time she arrived at the hospital, she was comatose. Her blood pressure had dropped so much that her body was already shutting down. She had pneumococcal pneumonia, the same bacterial infection that took the life of Muppets creator Jim Henson. One of its disastrous side effects is an activation of the body's clotting system, which causes the blood vessels to plug up. Because there was suddenly no blood flow to her hands or feet, she quickly developed gangrene in all four extremities. Two weeks after being admitted to the hospital, Jan's arms had to be amputated at mid-forearm and her legs at mid-shin.

Just before the surgery, she said she cried out, "Oh God, no! How can I live without arms and legs, feet or hands? Never walk again? Never play the trumpet, guitar, piano or any of the instruments I teach? I'll never be able to hug my sons or take care of them. Oh God, don't let me depend on others for the rest of my life!"

Six weeks after the amputations, as her dangling limbs healed, a doctor talked to Jan about prosthetics. She said Jan could learn to walk, drive a car, go back to school, even go back to teaching.

Jan found that hard to believe so she picked up her Bible. It fell open to Romans, chapter twelve, verse two: "Don't copy the behavior and customs of this world, but be a new and different person with a fresh newness in all you do and think. Then you will learn from your own experience how his ways will really satisfy you."

Jan thought about that—about being a new and different person—and she decided to give the prosthetics a try. With a walker strapped onto her forearms near the elbow and a therapist on either side, she could only wobble on her new legs for two to three minutes before she collapsed in exhaustion and pain.

Take it slowly, Jan said to herself. Be a new person in all that you do and think, but take it one step at a time.

The next day she tried on the prosthetic arms, a crude system of cables, rubber bands and hooks operated by a harness across the shoulders. By moving her shoulder muscles she was soon able to open and close the hooks to pick up and hold objects, and dress and feed herself.

Within a few months, Jan learned she could do almost everything she used to do—only in a new and different way.

"Still, when I finally got to go home after

four months of physical and occupational therapy, I was so nervous about what life would be like with my boys and me alone in the house. But when I got there, I got out of the car, walked up the steps to our house, hugged my boys with all my might, and we haven't looked back since."

As Jan and I continued to talk, Cody, who'd climbed out of the hotel pool, stood close to his mom with his arm around her shoulders. As she told me about her newly improved cooking skills, Cody grinned. "Yup," he said, "She's a better mom now than before she got sick, because now she can even flip pancakes!" Jan laughed like a woman who is blessed with tremendous happiness, contentment and unswerving faith in God.

Since our visit, Jan has completed a second college degree, this one in communications, and she is now an announcer for the local radio station. She also studied theology and has been ordained as the children's pastor at her church, the Triumphant Life Church in

Willmar. Simply put, Jan says, "I'm a new and different person, triumphant because of God's unending love and wisdom."

After meeting Jan, I was a new and different person as well. I learned to praise God for everything in my life that makes me new and different, whether it's struggling through one more part-time job to keep my kids in college, learning to be a grandmother for the first time or having the courage to end a relationship with a wonderful friend who just wasn't the right one for me.

Jan may not have real flesh-and-blood arms, legs, hands or feet, but that woman has more heart and soul than anyone I've ever met before or since. She taught me to grab on to every "new and different" thing that comes into my life with all the gusto I can muster... to live my life triumphantly.

~Patricia Lorenz
Chicken Soup for the Unsinkable Soul

and a slice of hot vanilla streusel cake, fresh out of the oven. She politely said, "No thank you" and as I watched her walk down the hall to her room, I felt slightly bad — but not as bad as I would have felt had I given her the last of my granola.

Dominique shows her love for Channel Road Inn's guests — and employees — through her baking. She works on her recipes for weeks to perfect them and is truly delighted when the guests "ooh and ah" over her creations. She is generous with most of her recipes, except for one. And that's okay, because this granola is so good, I'm betting one day it will be available in stores, and then our charming guest from Missouri, my girlfriend from Curves, and I can all eat Domi's granola to our heart's content!

~Rebecca Hill

"Of course. I'll be there around three. Is that okay?"

As they sat facing each other in the quiet of her small living room, Jim learned the reason for what he sensed in her voice. Martha told him that her doctor had just discovered a previously undetected tumor.

"He says I probably have six months to live." Martha's words were certainly serious, yet there was a definite calm about her.

"I'm so sorry to..." but before Jim could finish, Martha interrupted.

"Don't be. The Lord has been good. I have lived a long life. I'm ready to go. You know that."

"I know," Jim whispered with a reassuring nod.

"But I do want to talk with you about my funeral. I have been thinking about it, and there are things that I want."

The two talked quietly for a long time. They talked about Martha's favorite hymns, the passages of Scripture that had meant so much to her through the years, and the many memories they shared from the five years Jim had been with Central Church.

When it seemed that they had covered just about everything, Aunt Martie paused, looked up at Jim with a twinkle in her eye, and then added, "One more thing, Preacher. When they bury me, I want my old Bible in one hand and a fork in the other."

"A fork?" Jim was sure he had heard everything, but this caught him by surprise. "Why do you want to be buried with a fork?"

"I have been thinking about all of the church dinners and banquets that I attended through the years," she explained. "I couldn't begin to count them all. But one thing sticks in my mind.

"At those really nice get-togethers, when the meal was almost finished, a server or maybe the hostess would come by to collect the dirty dishes. I can hear the words now. Sometimes, at the best ones, somebody would lean over my shoulder and whisper, 'You can keep your fork.'

magazine. Her novel is entitled *Confessions of an Innkeeper*.

Mary Potter Kenyon cooks up soup and words in the Manchester, Iowa home she shares with her husband David and four of their eight children. Her writing appears in magazines, anthologies and the local newspaper. She is working with her agent on a book about couponing and blogs at marypotterkenyon.wordpress.com.

Linda O'Connell teaches in St. Louis, MO. Her humorous and inspirational essays have been published in twelve *Chicken Soup for the Soul* titles and many other regional and national publications. When Linda is wrist-deep in flour and sugar, she is knee-deep in thought. Linda blogs at lindaocon nell.blogspot.com.

Linda St.Cyr is a writer, blogger, activist, and short story author. When she isn't writing or raising her kids with her life partner, she is busy being vocal about feeding the hungry, sheltering the homeless, and bringing attention to human rights violations all over the world.

Diane Stark is a former elementary school teacher turned stay-at-home mom and freelance writer. She is a frequent contributor to the *Chicken Soup for the Soul* series. She is the author of *Teachers' Devotions to Go*. E-mail her at Diane Stark19@yahoo.com.

Linda C. Wright is an award-winning freelance writer and lives in Viera, FL. She's had many of her personal stories anthologized. Linda enjoys traveling, reading and photography. She is working on her second novel. E-mail her at lindacwright@ymail.com.

Jack has received many awards and honors, including three honorary doctorates and a Guinness World Records Certificate for having seven books from the *Chicken Soup for the Soul* series appearing on the New York Times bestseller list on May 24, 1998.

You can reach Jack at
www.jackcanfield.com.

Mark Victor Hansen is the co-founder of Chicken Soup for the Soul, along with Jack Canfield. He is a sought-after keynote speaker, bestselling author, and marketing maven. Mark's powerful messages of possibility, opportunity, and action have created powerful change in thousands of organizations and millions of individuals worldwide.

Mark is a prolific writer with many bestselling books in addition to the *Chicken Soup for the Soul* series. Mark has had a profound influence in the field of human potential through his library of audios, videos, and articles in the areas of big thinking, sales achievement, wealth building, publishing success, and personal and professional development. He is also the founder of the MEGA Seminar Series.

Mark has received numerous awards that honor his entrepreneurial spirit, philanthropic heart, and business acumen. He is a lifetime member of the Horatio Alger Association of Distinguished Americans.

You can reach Mark at
www.markvictorhansen.com.

Amy Newmark is Chicken Soup for the Soul's publisher and editor-in-chief, after a thirty-year career as a writer, speaker, financial analyst, and business executive in the worlds of finance and telecommunications. Amy is a *magna cum laude* graduate of Harvard College, where she majored in Portuguese, minored in French, and traveled extensively. She and her husband have four grown children.

After a long career writing books on telecommunications, voluminous financial reports, business plans, and corporate press releases, Chicken

Amy Newmark is Chicken Soup for the Soul's publisher and editor-in-chief, after a thirty-year career as a writer, speaker, financial analyst, and business executive in the worlds of finance and telecommunications. Amy is a *magna cum laude* graduate of Harvard College, where she majored in Portuguese, minored in French, and traveled extensively. She and her husband have four grown children.

After a long career writing books on telecommunications, voluminous financial reports, business plans, and corporate press releases, Chicken Soup for the Soul is a breath of fresh air for Amy. She has fallen in love with Chicken Soup for the Soul and its life-changing books, and really enjoys putting these books together for Chicken Soup for the Soul's wonderful readers. She has coauthored more than five dozen *Chicken Soup for the Soul* books and has edited another three dozen.

You can reach Amy with any questions or comments through webmaster@chickensoupforthe-soul.com and you can follow her on Twitter @amynewmark or @chickensoupsoul.

Chicken Soup for the Soul
Improving Your Life Every Day

Real people sharing real stories—for fifteen years. Now, Chicken Soup for the Soul has gone beyond the bookstore to become a world leader in life improvement. Through books, movies, DVDs, online resources and other partnerships, we bring hope, courage, inspiration and love to hundreds of millions of people around the world. Chicken Soup for the Soul's writers and readers belong to a one-of-a-kind global community, sharing advice, support, guidance, comfort, and knowledge.

Chicken Soup for the Soul stories have been translated into more than forty languages and can be found in more than one hundred countries. Every day, millions of people experience a Chicken Soup for the Soul story in a book, magazine, newspaper or online. As we share our life experiences through these stories, we offer hope, comfort and inspiration to one another. The stories travel from person to person, and from country to country, helping to improve lives everywhere.

Share with Us

We all have had Chicken Soup for the Soul moments in our lives. If you would like to share your story or poem with millions of people around the world, go to chickensoup.com and click on "Submit Your Story." You may be able to help another reader, and become a published author at the same time. Some of our past contributors have launched writing and speaking careers from the publication of their stories in our books!

Our submission volume has been increasing steadily—the quality and quantity of your submissions has been fabulous. We only accept story submissions via our website. They are no longer accepted via mail or fax.

To contact us regarding other matters, please

send us an e-mail through webmaster@chicken-soupforthesoul.com, or fax or write us at:

Chicken Soup for the Soul
P.O. Box 700
Cos Cob, CT 06807-0700
Fax: 203-861-7194

One more note from your friends at Chicken Soup for the Soul: Occasionally, we receive an unsolicited book manuscript from one of our readers, and we would like to respectfully inform you that we do not accept unsolicited manuscripts and we must discard the ones that appear.